To Brian Yass
Best regards,
George Henry Notz

Poetry for Adults and Children

Poetry for Adults and Children

George Henry Kotz

VANTAGE PRESS
New York

FIRST EDITION

Published by Vantage Press, Inc.
419 Park Ave. South, New York, NY 10016

Manufactured in the United States of America
ISBN: 978-0-533-16092-1

Library of Congress Catalog Card No: 2008905914

0 9 8 7 6 5 4 3 2 1

To Dorothy (Ebert) Kotz, my mother,
and to my fifteen brothers and sisters,
to my wife, Nancy,
and our three children

Contents

Poetry for Adults and Children

Words Becoming Poems

My mind is filled with many words,
Like a large flock of migrating birds,
Looking for a safe place to rest,
To find a mate, then build a nest.
Once complete, the nest becomes a home,
Where all combined will form a poem.
Now the words all fit just right,
Once again they will all take flight.
Searching for another nesting place,
Where many words have a different face.

A Special Birthday

On December the twenty-fifth of every year,
We celebrate the birthday of one we hold so dear.
He is the child Jesus, whom God the Father chose,
To be born and place in a manger,
Wrapped in swaddling clothes.
He didn't come to us as a hero with a crowd gone wild,
He came as a gentle, pure, sweet, loving child.
He was here on earth for a very short stay,
His purpose was to show us the way.
Two thousand years have already gone by,
We celebrate Christmas, but many know not why.

Just a Thought

Have you hugged someone you love today,
Or taken a moment to silently pray?
If you are someone who doesn't believe in prayer,
Have you at least shown a loved one that you care?
If you are a person who doesn't believe in love,
Or that there is a God above,
Then maybe it's time for you to look around,
And you'll see the everyday miracles that still abound.

The Spoken Word

This is America land of the free,
Where people came to escape from tyranny.
We chose English as our speaking word,
Since our country was born it's the language heard.
Now there are some who wish to change this rule,
Making Spanish our speaking tool.
Our forefathers came from many foreign lands,
Speaking a foreign language
Carrying belongings in their hands.
They had to learn English in order to live,
In this great nation that has so much to give.
It is a plus to know another spoken word,
But if you choose America, English is our spoken word.

Freedom's Price

To make a country as free as ours,
Took fighting men and women millions of hours.
It was because of will power and determination,
That we became one, together as a nation.
The price of freedom certainly came high,
At a terrible cost of life, so many had to die.
People will ask, "Why must it be done this way?"
There is no answer, it seems to be the human way.
If people don't learn to see eye to eye,
The price of freedom will always be high.

The Real War

Let's play war, let's go wild,
I said one day when I was a child.
I shoot you as you crawl under the bed,
Then you lay still, you play dead.
Boy! This is such a lot of fun,
Naturally I have no bullets in my gun.
I could play like this every day,
Shooting you as you come my way.
Now into a man I have grown,
This is a real war, I'm on my own.
It is no longer a lot of fun,
Bullets fly from a genuine gun.
There's no more crawling under the bed,
I'm crawling on my belly in mud instead.
I must aim and shoot to survive,
And pray to God that I get home alive.

Count Me Blessed

I cannot walk or run like you,
Nor bend down to tie my shoe.
I cannot stand up by myself,
To reach for something on a shelf.
My body is not what you would call the norm,
It is not built like most, it has a different form.
I ask God why, "Why me, God, why?"
I then say to myself, "How Dare You Cry."
Do not question Him, my God above,
Who shows compassion through His love.
He has surely blessed me, He is kind,
He has given me a healthy heart and mind.

In Loving Memory

There is a parade headed this way,
The reason for this, it's Memorial Day.
For those who don't know,
This is not a mere show,
It's our way of remembering those who once were alive,
And gave their lives so that we could survive,
They too shared a song,
As they marched along,
Headed for battle in some faraway land,
They too heard the sound of a brass band.
All music and songs were stilled,
As so many of them were killed.
They shall be remembered through the years,
By their loved ones who have shed so many tears.

The American Veteran

Hello America! Remember me?
I fought bravely to keep you free.
I am the veteran who answered your call,
To protect and defend you, one and all.
I am the veteran who spent months to years,
Defending a nation filled with many fears.
Would the enemy invade our land,
Forcing civilians to take a stand?
I did not let that come about,
I made sure to keep the enemy out.
I fought valiantly during the day and through the night,
With my heart and soul I gave it all my might.
There were thousands of others like me,
Who fought for our country in the air, on land and sea.
Many brave souls never returned alive,
We the fortunate ones still survive.
Some of us came through it all unscathed,
Other shave scars they will take to the grave.
Dear America, please never forget,
Your all-giving protector, your loving vet.

A Christmas of Plenty

'Twas the day after Christmas and all through the house,
Not a creature was stirring, not even the mouse.
Their bellies were filled with food and drink,
Even the dishes still sat in the sink.
The presents which were wrapped with such loving care,
Were scattered here and there and everywhere.
Even the mouse ate so much that he grew fat,
He wouldn't be able to move if he had to run from the cat.
Come to think of it, the cat wouldn't be able
To catch the mouse,
For the cat had his fill, like everyone else in the house.
It's fun to celebrate Christmas with presents and tree,
In this great country America, where the people are free.

A World in Trouble

The trouble with the world today,
Not enough people take time to pray.
Too many minds are filed with lust,
Whatever happened to "In God We Trust"?
Where are all the hearts sincere,
To help make love re-appear?
What happened to the brotherhood of man?
Have we turned it into some ugly sham?
The trouble with the world today,
Is not up to me to say.
If people will just look around,
They will see that love can still be found.

The Confession of a Drug Addict

I carry this monkey on my back,
I am hopelessly hooked on crack.
Nothing I do is on the level,
I am controlled by this devil.
I am not to be trusted,
In a matter of time I'll be busted.
Every word I speak is a lie,
Each day I live just slips by.
I use this drug that kills my brain,
I am throwing my life down the drain.
I am not a bad person, it is my will that is weak,
I cannot control myself, people call me a sneak.
I never have money to pay for a meal,
My habit has forced me to go out and steal.
My life has no meaning unless I am high,
I guess I am living just one great big lie.

Innocent Children

What do little children say,
As they spend their time at play?
Do they realize they're not kin,
Because of the color of their skin?
Their innocent minds are pure,
Of this you can be sure.
They share their toys,
These girls and boys.
They even kiss and hug each other.
In innocent love like sister and brother.
They do not yet know how to hate,
Nor know the words used to berate.
Little children learn from others,
Mostly from their fathers and mothers.

The Falling Rain

As I sit here by my window pane,
Looking at the falling rain.
I notice a sky so dark and grey,
It's such a dank and dreary day.
Now as I stay here and brood,
I begin to ponder my melancholy mood.
I have allowed my thoughts to go astray,
On this wet, cold and rainy day.
The moisture laden clouds must burst,
So that Mother Nature may quench her thirst.
All life upon this planet depends on rain,
That's why we must have dreary days again and again.

A Look at Us

While everything seems sunny and bright,
Our dreams somehow just take flight.
Why don't our many wishes materialize,
Instead of meeting a disappointing demise?
Living in a world full of stress and strife,
Maybe we expect too much of life.
Would it be better if we slow down the pace
Could this be a way to make the world a better place?
Many people set their goals too high,
And when they fail, they wonder why.
If we count our blessings and cut out the greed,
Many of our dreams will come true indeed.

A Sudden Awakening

The easiest thing for me to do,
Is to criticize and find fault with you.
Can't you hear, don't you know,
Boy oh boy, you annoy me so?
When I speak, you don't listen to me,
What the heck can the matter be?
Suddenly I take a good look at myself,
Is it possible that I've been fooling myself?
The hardest thing for me to see,
Is that the real fault lies in me.

The First Years of Life

A child is born into this world,
As pure as the new-fallen snow.
What will become of this child,
Not one person can possibly know.
The mother is constantly there,
With her tender loving care.
As sure as there is a sky above,
This baby is showered with total love.
Along with joy comes laughter and tears,
Which is normal during the early years.
Then this child receives a learning tool,
And enters into a whole new world called school.
During these years this child gets to know others,
Who are also loved by their fathers and mothers.

Freedom Without Fear

Thank you Lord for giving me,
This land of hope and liberty.
A place to live and call my home,
Where I can sit in peace and write this poem.
Where I am allowed to speak my piece,
Without fear of retribution by secret police,
Where I can vote for whom I choose,
And still be free, win or lose.
Where I can worship God in my own way,
And not be told that I'm not allowed to pray.
These freedoms I enjoy, that are wonderfully nice,
Were obtained by many who paid the ultimate price.
They fought for liberty and justice for all,
That's why we must be alert and always stand tall.

The Symbol of Our Land

The beautiful bald eagle, a magnificent bird of prey,
Soars high above the earth all through the day.
A strong but gentle bird that can become extremely fierce,
Attacking another animal's hide,
Its talons can easily pierce.
The bald eagle excels above all other large birds,
By showing courage and fearlessness far beyond words.
If you know of America's history,
Now you can understand,
Why the beautiful bald eagle is the symbol of our land.

Thoughts of a Dying Addict

Thinking not of others, the only one was me,
Everywhere I'd go, it was just my world to see.
No one else mattered much at all,
To me life just meant having a ball.
It only mattered if I had fun,
Now my life is almost done.
Please give me some time Lord!

I don't really want to go,
I need time to let everyone know.
How sincerely sorry I am,
I'm a lost and lonely man.
I've hurt so many as I went along,
I wish I could right what I've done wrong.
Please give me some time Lord!

Back to Basics

Why do people continue to hate one another,
Total strangers, as well as sister and brother?
What is this sickness that affects the human race,
And continues at an alarming pace?
As each generation produces a brighter mind,
They don't seem to know how to be kind.
People don't care about the Golden Rule,
Instead they play each other for the fool.
What has happened to "Do Unto Others,"
That was taught by our fathers and mothers?
When people turn their backs on God,
They become confused and rather odd.
Even children attending our schools,
Are just ignoring the basic rules.
Disrespect for authority is the order of the day,
If some disgruntled students don't have their way.
The time has come for us to open our eyes,
Lest we all meet a very sad demise.

A Treasure of Love

May your life be filled with a treasure of love,
May you always be blessed by the Lord above.
A wish for you and yours a happy life,
With as little as possible stress and strife.
As we live our life we cannot always please,
May you live yours sharing love with ease.

Persevere in Life

Anyone who has love in their heart,
Will never see their world fall apart.
This is not an easy life,
As we deal with disappointment and strife.
Life goes on and we do our best,
God constantly puts us to the test.
As we walk along we sometimes fall,
Just get up; brush off; and then stand tall.

Sensible Drinking

Here I sit, munching pretzels, drinking beer,
With all the people that I hold dear
We gather here to socialize and have some fun,
It's a relaxing time for each and every one.
Often times someone drinks too much brew,
We all know that this is nothing new.
A person in this condition can become an ass,
Upon becoming sober, could crawl into the glass.
So, my advice to all you lovely folks,
Drink with care, don't be a wheel without spokes.

Beauty and the Beast

It was on a beautiful peaceful September morn,
When terror struck and our hearts were torn.
Standing tall and firm, two stately towers,
Engineering marvels we proudly called ours.
The majestic twins stood high in the New York sky,
The way they died just makes me cry.
Hundreds of police and firefighters responded to distress,
They lost their lives, leaving us with emptiness.
The thousands of people working and living inside,
Did so with a feeling of peace and pride.
So many of these poor souls are also no more,
The hearts of their loved ones are broken and sore.
Hundreds of people on four separate flights,
Never suspected the outcome, such horrible sights.
Mighty airliners turned into weapons of destruction,
By the devil terrorists who needed no introduction.

The Firefighter's Job

There's a person trapped inside,
Will I be able to save his hide?
As I crawl through the smoke and flame,
I don't look for praise and fame.
My job is to put the fire out,
And make sure to get the victims out.
I am one of the firefighting men in blue,
Who are here to protect every one of you,
From the awful smoke and flame,
That will choke you, kill and maim.
Firefighters are who we are,
Fighting fires, near and afar.
Anytime, be it night or day,
Whether we volunteer or work for pay.
We are always at your beck and call,
To help and protect you, one and all.

Freedom Forever

This is America land of the free, home of the brave,
We don't cause terror, then flee and hide in a cave.
We don't have to run and hide,
We know that God is on our side.
Our belief is in a cause that is just,
To protect our freedom is a must.
This freedom we cherish was never bought,
To obtain it, many a fierce battle was fought.
Anyone who thinks that they can take it away.
Will feel our wrath, and with their life will pay.

An Easter Wish

May this poem,
We send to your home,
Bring the blessing of the Lord above,
As well as our deepest feelings of love.
Let us rejoice in the risen Lord,
And ask His blessing as a just reward.
May we be guided by His Holy Word,
And may our fervent prayers be heard.
May the Easter celebration
Bring peace to every nation.

America, How I Love Thee

I

America, how I love thee,
Sweet, sweet land of liberty.
You open your arms to the world's oppressed,
Not always receiving the very best.
Still, you continue on in a loving way,
In spite of those trying to cause dismay.
You persevere in your righteous cause,
Even when you incur some flaws.
You are the envy of many who don't understand,
How you can welcome people of another land.

II

America, how I love thee,
Home of people who are free.
You have had your share of grief,
"In God We Trust," is your belief.
Yet, there are those living in this world,
Who wish to see your freedom spoiled.
You will never let this happen to you,
Because your love of God and man is true.
Being part of you, Oh! How I am blest,
My dear America, you are the best.

Angry Mother Earth

I am the most beautiful of God's creations,
Millions of years old, host to many civilizations.
So many have come and gone,
Still I manage to carry on.
I am blest with all it takes to support life,
Yet I witness so much terror and strife.
I can bear it when my continents change,
Even if it makes me feel strange.
What had recently come about,
Is a pain that makes me shout.
Living upon me is a creature called man,
Who doesn't seem to give a damn.
He builds machines to help him toil,
He uses my blood he calls oil.
Now he is fighting to suck my blood dry,
His actions make me want to cry.
He will kill himself by becoming sick,
Then I will be rid of this monstrous tick.

The Speck in the Vastness of Space

I am but a speck in the vastness of space,
No one knows just when I became this place.
This place teeming with life, called earth,
Constantly changing and growing since birth.
I am an absolute marvel created by God,
Although the people I harbor are rather odd.
I give them my riches and food,
In return they treat me terribly rude.
They kill one another fighting for land,
Be it a beautiful forest, or just plain sand.
They are never satisfied with all that I give,
So that they may harmoniously and peacefully live.
If they continue to go on at this foolish pace,
It will kill me, the speck in the vastness of space.

I Love the U.S.A.

The United States of America,
The name is music to my ears.
The United States of America,
My homeland for many years.
This land is a special place,
Within, live people of every race.
We came from all around the world,
To escape from tyranny and freedom spoiled.
We choose the people who govern our land,
Through free elections, we all lend a hand.
We believe that all people should be free,
A reality that dictators do not want to see.
We were given by God, a land of riches and beauty,
To share with others, we feel is our duty.
To do what is right, is our basic belief,
Not accomplished without some grief.
We've been involved in many a terrible fight,
We always fought for what is right.
Thousands of people died defending our cause,
Too bad it had to be through many wars.
In the future, may it be done a different way
In the meantime, I still love the U.S.A.

G.I.s in Saddam's Home Town

I

You better watch out, you'll never get out,
Our well trained G.I.s will ferret you out.
G.I.s are now in your home town.
They will search while you are sleeping,
They will search while you are awake.
We know that you are no good,
We must get rid of you for goodness sake.

II

You were finally found in a hole in the ground,
All alone, without your followers around.
They examined you, and checked you for lice,
They found your list, and are checking it twice.
We must certainly say,
Your terrible crimes did not pay.
G.I.s have caught you in your home town.

Will We Ever Learn?

Thousand of years have come and gone,
Yet wars and destruction continue on.
What is wrong with the human race,
That compels us to keep up this pace?
Can't we find a way to settle scores,
Instead of always having wars?
We spent time and money fighting disease,
Then settle our differences by killing with ease.
This behavior seems so very sad,
Could it be that we are all a bit mad?

Wealth Is Not Everything

If it's a pot of gold you are looking for,
Or a room full of riches, piled to the door.
You can awaken from your impossible dream,
Face reality, riches are not what they seem.
True, they help us put bread on the table,
To feel you only need wealth is a fable.
If it's just wealth you think you need,
You'll do better by helping others in need.

When

Life is but a fleeting moment in time,
Why not treat it like something sublime?
Our short stay here on earth,
Goes by swiftly following our birth.
The four seasons each come and go,
Yet many people never get to know,
The awesome beauty of our world,
The many places not yet spoiled.
We live on a planet teeming with life,
Yet there continues ongoing strife.
It's all about having material things,
Not stopping to hear how a bird sings.
The ongoing march off to war,
When will we see it no more?
When is hatred of each other going to cease,
So that we can all live together in peace?

Life Is Not Forever

Yesterday is gone, today is here, tomorrow is nigh,
How very swiftly the days go by.
I sit here and think about yesterday,
When I was a small child at play.
I didn't have a care in the world,
Innocent in mind, not even spoiled.
To me the whole world looked bold,
I never thought I would grow old.
Life and adventure would go on and on,
No youth thinks it will ever be gone.
Finally the day came when I realized,
Life is not forever, eventually everyone dies.

Words never cure the hurt,
They can only soothe the profound pain.

Did You Ever?

Did you ever watch a tree sway as the wind blows,
Or stop to examine and smell a beautiful rose?
Did you ever watch a honey bee in its determination,
Collecting nectar from flowers,
Thereby causing pollination?
Did you ever listen on a quiet night in spring,
And hear the beautiful mocking bird sing?
Did you ever catch a beautiful butterfly,
Release it, and watch it fly high in the sky?
Did you ever watch a bird go on endlessly without rest,
Spending many hours on building its nest?
Did you ever watch the clouds in the sky,
Change into different forms as they pass by?
Did you ever see a rainbow after a rain,
When the sun begins to shine again?
Did you ever think arranging all these events is hard?
It's not, you see, they are all being arranged by God.

Nature's Mystery

Nothing compares to nature's beauty and power,
Or when she is angry, escapes her wrath.
She can produce a very beautiful flower,
Or wreak havoc, threatening everything in her path.
We have invented ways and gone to great length,
To minimize damage caused by her awesome strength.
We depend on nature's gifts to sustain life,
And have to adjust to the four seasons.
Will we, in our experience of ongoing strife,
In our infinite thinking, ever figure out her reasons?

Finding a Way

How can anyone say, "We can't find a way,
To have peace in the world, to prevent freedom spoiled"?
If you make up your mind, try not to be blind,
You can open your eyes, ignore he who belies.
Negative thinking can only lead to defeat,
Always think positive, be forever discreet.
We all have a free will to decide and choose,
Sometimes we make mistakes and lose.
We must be forever on our guard,
Even if we find it extremely hard.
In this day and age it has become a must,
To put all our efforts into a cause that is just.
If we remain loyal to our cause, making no error,
We will defeat our enemy, ending all terror.

The Light of Hope—P.O.W., M.I.A.

As we gaze out upon the mist,
We know not if you still exist.
You disappeared while doing your part,
And left us all with an empty heart.
Our thoughts are with you as we pray,
That you will return to us some day.
Even if this does not come about,
We will never let our hopes give out.
We pray to God that you did survive,
And will return to us while still alive.
In the meantime, while you are gone,
The light of hope will still be on.

To a Precious Daughter

(To Theresa and Tammy Ann)

I planted a seed in your mother's womb,
From that seed a precious daughter did bloom.
It didn't matter if you were a girl or boy,
You gave us many moments of joy.
Often as the darkness of night arrives,
My head on my pillow, I close my eyes.
As my conscious mind drifts into sleep,
I think of those precious moments I'll forever keep.
If it were possible to re-live the past,
I wouldn't have to! My love for you will forever last.

Will They Ever Learn?

Who are these creatures who create great marvels,
These creatures gifted with a fabulous brain,
Who can also cause much grief and pain?
They have split the atom that has enormous power,
If wrongly used, could destroy all in an hour.
They have been given a life to in harmony live,
Yet harmony escapes like sand through a sieve.
When will these creatures, called the human race,
Learn to share and love, in this beautiful place?
They have been endowed with their own free will,
Yet, instead of sharing and loving, choose to kill.
Will they ever learn that crime and hate don't pay,
That respect and love is the proper way?

The Promise

You say you love me now,
Will you show me how,
How very much you care,
That you will always be there?
Through thick or thin,
If we lose or win,
Will you be always at my side,
With ever loving pride?
Sometimes love can become lame,
Will your thoughts still be the same?
Can you handle stress and strife,
As we travel the road of life?
If you feel that you will always be true,
Then I promise to spend my life loving you.

Try Love, Not Hate

We split the atom which has enormous power,
That could destroy us all within the hour.
We are gifted with a fabulous brain,
Yet cause each other enormous pain.
If we humans created by God above,
Would only change hate to love.
All the war and terror would cease,
Then we could all begin to live in peace.
If we don't change our ways,
There will not be many peaceful days.

Never Before

Never before have I met someone so sweet,
Never before has someone knocked me off my feet.
It was a that very moment that I knew,
I must spend the rest of my life with you.
Never before have I felt quite like this,
Wanting to give you a loving tender kiss.
When my fast beating heart took flight,
I knew I had fallen in love at first sight.

The Source of Life

The sun sets and the day is gone,
We give it no thought as life goes on.
Night arrives with it shadowy veil,
We can hear the song of a nightingale.
Darkness never lasts for long,
Soon there is another dawn.
This event has taken place,
Since planet earth appeared in space.
Life on earth could not have begun,
Without energy derived from the sun.

Seventy-Four and Counting

Now that I have reached age seventy-four,
I hope the Lord gives me many more.
All I can do, is have faith in Him,
Try to do good, and steer away from sin.
I can only hope that He hears my plea,
I'll be the best person that I can be.
He hasn't always answered my prayers,
I will not complain, by splitting hairs.
My life here on earth is in His hands,
Slowly ebbing like the shifting sands,
When all of life's suffering takes its toll,
I pray that the good Lord takes my soul.

Advice to a Child

My dear child you are just starting your life,
As times goes by you'll learn all about strife.
There will be times when all will be swell,
Sadly, you'll find that life can be hell.
Sometimes you'll think you know it all,
To continue that thought is a bad call.
You must not allow others to control your mind,
You should be respectful, truthful and kind.
You many experience times when all falls apart,
Put the pieces together, get a new start.
You may think life is very hard.
Not if you have faith in yourself and God.

Dreams

When I was a child I dreamed of Santa and toys,
I dreamed of playing with other girls and boys.
I hated having to go off to school to learn,
I counted the days till the end of each term.
How important education is; I had no clue,
I impatiently waited for school to be through.
At last I graduated, no more school,
I'm glad I hung in there, now I'm no fool.
Time is fleeting, just passing us by,
It just happens, don't ask me, why?
Now I have children of my own,
They don't like school and want to stay home.
I tell them about my childhood schemes,
How I thought life was nothing but dreams.
I tell them how important it is to finish school,
Now they will grow up being no one's fool.

A Fleeting Moment

I saw you across the crowded street,
My poor heart just skipped a beat.
Something that I can't explain,
Placed a thought in my brain.
Cast everything else aside,
Cross over to the other side.
I can't go against the traffic light,
Now you've gone from my sight.
The light changed, I looked around,
You were nowhere to be found.
A meeting between you and me,
Just wasn't meant to be.

The Error of Terror

What fools these terrorists be,
Beyond their nose they do not see.
To live in peace becomes a bore,
Another dispute; they go to war.
They claim that they are civilized,
Some do good, they are despised.
This is a group that believes in terror,
This belief of theirs is in total error.
History proves they'll not succeed,
In carrying out their evil deed.
In their mind they think they're right,
That causing havoc wins their fight.
They are filled with a seething hate,
Which will eventually seal their fate.
They despise people of the western world,
And wish their lifestyle to be spoiled.
We know that this will never be,
Terrorists don't know the meaning of liberty.

Bullet

Alone I am a rather harmless one,
I have an accomplice called a gun
The gun and I are man's creation,
Found around the world, in every nation.
On land, on sea, and in the air,
The gun and I are quite a pair.
We are on the side of good, and bad,
Either way, we have made people sad.
Gun and I have killed so very many,
Without gun, I couldn't kill any.
If we could simply go away,
Man would kill another way.

Katrina

The rain came, the wind came,
Together they formed a hurricane.
It was the year two thousand and five,
When hurricane Katrina decided to arrive.
She picked Louisiana to do her worst,
The place was flooded when the levees burst.
The devastation was far beyond belief,
So many people were shattered in grief.
Roofs blown away, ripped from the beams,
The storm shattered lifelong dreams.
Families were separated, children, husbands and wives.
Many more unfortunate victims lost their lives.
People were drowned, young and old.
When the levees could no longer hold.
We sent a spacecraft to the moon with a gallant crew,
Being able to tame a storm like Katrina, we haven't a clue.

Our Unsung Heroes

They all stepped up to join the fight,
For a cause that we all know is right.
They felt that they could lend a hand,
To keep the enemy from our land.
They fought many battles so fierce and hard,
These unsung heroes placed their faith in God.
They believed that people should be free,
That all should live in total liberty.
They heard the sound of freedom's call,
Then became our unsung heroes, one and all.
It wasn't many years since their birth,
Now they all lie beneath the earth.

Just Arrived

So tiny, so precious and sweet,
From your head down to your feet.
Such pretty eyes, ears and nose,
Delicate arms, hands, legs and toes.
You know nothing of heartache and strife,
You are such an innocent brand new life.
You just left your loving mother's womb,
You're a beautiful flower in full bloom.
You are the star; you have the power,
This my dear child, is your shining hour.

Believe in God

What fools we mortals be,
Beyond our nose we do not see.
We worry about the end of the world,
Yet we continue to become embroiled.
If we could for just one moment realize,
Each day is the end for those who meet their demise.
The rest of us are left to continue life,
Some live in peace, some live in strife.
Most have not a clue since birth,
Just why we live upon this planet earth.
To go too deep in thought asking, "Why?" is sad,
You will not find answers, you'll go mad.
Instead of becoming confused and odd,
Maybe it's best for all to believe in God.

Health Is Wealth

As we live each day of our life,
We encounter much stress and strife.
Most of the time we don't think to pray,
As we go busily on our way.
The precious days come and go,
What tomorrow will bring we never know.
We take so may things for granted,
Not realizing the seeds of neglect we planted.
Taking care of ourselves and our health,
Is more rewarding than a mountain of wealth.

Understanding Life

Life is an ongoing mystery,
Before long it becomes history.
Therefore we should put in our mind,
The thought to always be kind.
At times life seems very hard to bear,
We may feel that no one seems to care.
This is when we must search our soul,
Do not let confusion take its toll.
Surely everyone will have a different way,
To have in mind what they wish to say.
If we could put ourselves in another's place,
Maybe our life would have a different face.

Some Facts of Life

We humans are born with different colors and races,
We have many different shapes and faces.
If you could look underneath our skin,
You would see that we are all the same within.
The biggest difference is in our mind,
Some of us are cruel, and some are kind.
A fact of life that is so very sad,
Many people throughout the world are bad.
Thank God that the majority of us are good,
And live our lives the way we should.
Treating one another with respect and love,
Is the way to please the Lord above.

Stirrings of Spring

As I walk through the forest in the springtime dawn,
I catch a glimpse of a female deer and her fawn.
There are hundreds of trees all around,
Just a few months ago there was snow on the ground.
One wonders how all of the animals managed to survive,
Now the beautiful forest is beginning to come alive.
The opening of buds on the trees has begun,
Coaxed by the warming rays of the sun.
There is awesome beauty seen all around,
The many birds are singing their mating sound.

Ode to the Horse

The horse is such a magnificent beast,
Ode to this animal is saying the least.
For centuries the horse has helped to advance mankind,
On the farm it toiled, pulling a plow behind.
For centuries man tamed and bred this beautiful beast,
Sad to say, when times were hard,
Horseflesh became a feast.
Humans can travel just so far on foot
Much less carry freight,
A horse can endure much longer,
While carrying heavy weight.
Man and horse have worked together,
Enduring many different kinds of weather.
Times have changed,
The horse has been replaced by machines,
Ode to this beast, to whom we owe so much, by all means.

The Four Chaplains

The incident took place on the troop ship *Dorchester*
During World War Two,
It involved four chaplains on board,
Three Christians, the other a Jew.
Sailing in the North Atlantic with U-boats lurking in the frigid waters,
There were nine hundred passengers living in extremely cramped quarters.
It was on February third, nineteen hundred forty-three,
When the *Dorchester* ran out of luck,
A well-aimed torpedo from a lurking enemy German U-boat struck,
Those final hours became a most terrible nightmare,
There was total terror and chaos almost everywhere.
The four chaplains handed out life jackets until there were no more,
Then they linked their arms together,
Singing praises to God, the Chaplains four.
As the doomed *Dorchester* slipped silently into the sea,
These brave chaplains and those left aboard,
Passed into eternity.
Out of nine hundred passengers,
One-third of them survived,
From this tragic incident, deep love and unity
Has been derived.

You Never Know

He is wearing two different shoes to protect his feet,
As he shuffles his way along the city street.
Pushing a shopping cart carrying discarded cans,
Surely in the past he must have had other plans.
He once gave two people the utmost joy,
He was their precious, beautiful baby boy.
Something went terribly wrong in this man's life,
That caused the loss of his battle with ongoing strife.
Never look at him as though he is less than you,
Your future could change you that way too.

How Fragile We Are

The waves seemingly in anger smash at the shore,
You are in my way, you will be hit with many more.
This seems to be what the powerful waves have to say,
As I walk along the water's edge and feel
The resulting spray.
I look out to the horizon and see the rays of the sun,
Dancing upon the surface of the ocean as if becoming one.
The two of them have such awesome power,
As they continue in determination hour after hour.
If this ongoing occurrence would cease to be,
Our planet Earth would die and so would we.

A Sad Observation

A world full of people who are running amuck,
All they want is riches and the almighty buck.
There is no more mention of "In God We Trust,"
So many minds are filled with hate and lust.
Our youth are growing up in a disrespectful way,
They have not been taught by their peers to pray.
Wherever you go there is addiction to sex and drugs,
Stealing from others, many have become low life thugs.
Will this madness and mayhem ever end,
So that our once beautiful world will begin to mend?

How Swift Is Life!

How swift is life,
Half glee, half strife.
From leaving the womb,
To becoming full bloom.
'Tis such a beautiful dawn,
Cherish it before it is gone.
Like the new day's light,
It soon becomes night.
Before we can figure out this mystery.
We have just become history.

Live with Direction

Be it better that I die for a just cause,
Rather than to die without a set course.
A man that has no direction in life,
Would fare better by falling upon a knife.
For living a life not as a free man,
Is as bad as living without a plan.
Life must be lived with a certain goal,
Or it is lived like a body without a soul.
Just existing in time, day after day,
Most certainly is not the way.

The Cycle of Life

Not a day goes by that a baby doesn't cry,
Not a moment goes by that someone doesn't die.
With the passing of night follows the dawn,
It is a new day and another baby is born.
Ongoing is the cycle of life,
A combination of gladness and strife.
Like the cycle of the four seasons,
Will we ever figure out the reasons?
We think that we know so much,
But we are still way out of touch.
Maybe it's best that we don't know it all,
Could it be that some mystery is better for all?

A Blink of the Eye

As a child, who looks ahead,
Another day gone, we go to bed?
As the sun sets in the west,
We prepare for another night's rest.
We drift into another night of dreams,
How swift night passes, so it seems.
We awaken to a brand new dawn,
We blink our eyes, and another day is gone.
It is when the years have passed,
That we realize, they have gone so fast.
We have lived our lives in different ways,
Now we look back at our childhood days.
It is so sad to know that they are gone,
Time has come for a new generation to carry on.

A Just Cause

To protect and defend our land of riches and beauty,
Is each and every loyal American's duty.
So many before us have worked very hard,
To nurture our land so provided by God.
At the present time, living here are people with no belief,
Their negative mentality is causing
Many good people grief.
Every American who loves our precious land,
Must make up their mind and take a stand.
We must never forget our cause that is just,
To overcome despots and traitors is a definite must.

A Sad Fact

There was a time when delicious odors filled the air,
Today; sadly they are no longer there.
The smell of baking bread,
Apple blossoms overhead.
A gentle breeze would transport them along,
A whiff now and then, all day long.
Today these odors are overwhelmed by pollution,
No one has come up with a solution.
Soot and oil fumes fill the air,
Not very many people seem to care.

The Bumpy Life of a Frog

I am a frog and I have this problem,
Every time I hop I hit my bottom.
I wish that I had been given a fair shake,
And been born a slithering, legless snake.
You may say that I get there in a hop, skip and a jump,
But it sure hurts my bottom as I go bumpity bump.
It's certainly not easy being a frog,
My only relief is when I sit on a log.
So much my dear folks, for my tale of woe,
I must be off now, hitting my bottom as I go.

Angels of Mercy

God bless the people who become a nurse,
Without these angels we would feel so much worse.
They work tirelessly putting in many hours,
In spite of sickness and tragedy dedication never sours.
They are the unsung heroes of the medical world,
Who never complain, no matter how hard they've toiled.
They are there for sick people in need of care,
We thank them for always being there.

When Will the World Be Free?

How many wars will it take,
Before people of the world come awake?
How much more blood will be spilled,
As millions of more people are killed?
So many have already met their fate,
The victims of so much ongoing hate.
When will everyone open their eyes,
And prevent civilization from a sad demise?
To prevent this ongoing senseless madness,
That causes untold grief and sadness.
One must take a long deep look at self,
Side stepping all riches and wealth.
Realize once and for all, peace begins in me,
Only then will the whole world be free.

Harvesting the Oak Tree

Sprouting from an acorn out of the soil,
Began the long life of the mighty oak.
Growing continually, winter, spring, summer and fall,
Becoming taller and stronger under nature's cloak.
Strongly rooted in one place upon the earth,
Providing refuge for wildlife, especially birds.
Birds travel miles away from their origin of birth,
The mighty oak cannot move on like the birds.
Standing tall and stately, reaching for the sky,
This mighty oak will soon change its form.
It will be harvested for lumber by and by,
And become a piece of furniture before long.

Beautiful Flowers

Thank God for giving us beautiful flowers,
They give people joy for a great many hours.
To bring cheer to someone who is sick,
A bouquet of flowers will do the trick.
We sit down at the dinner table to eat,
Looking at a vase of flowers is really neat.
In a flower bed surrounded by grass,
They certainly add a touch of class.
Their succulent nectar is food for bees,
Who build their hives in holes in trees.
Flowers surround us from our time of birth,
Until our time is complete, here on earth.

Smile

We all have something that we can give away,
It's called a smile that can make someone's day.
It doesn't cost one single cent,
Just a friendly greeting well spent.
It takes just one moment of our time,
And can change the down hearted into feeling fine.
So lift your chin up off the floor,
And continue to smile some more.
It can be done with apparent ease,
Like "God Bless You" when you hear someone sneeze.

August Outside Consolation

Jets flying high in the sky,
Automobiles constantly driving by.
Speed boats gliding across the bay,
The weather is gorgeous this August day.
Trees completely full of green leaves,
Sway majestically in the gentle breeze.
Children playing and chasing one another,
Under the watchful eyes of their mother.
Birds continue to fly nervously overhead,
Then settle on the ground to eat bits of bread.
We can see a rock garden, and a waterfall running,
Below is a pond with goldfish swimming.
Pretty flowers and shrubs all around,
Overlooking all, a statue of Our Lady can be found.

A World of Peace

As I sit here on a peaceful sunny day,
Watching a small child at play.
My thoughts slip back to days that used to be,
I can see a child that once was me.
So many years have come and gone,
Thankfully my life continued on.
This small child is just beginning life,
And has not experienced heartache and strife.
I think to myself, how nice it would be,
If children could grow up in a world of harmony.
Where people of all religions, colors and races,
Could respect and love one another in all places.
A world where all hate and wars will cease,
A world where all people live in peace.

Thoughts to a Friend

The warmth of your friendship
Gives me a pleasing feeling,
Your generous outgoing nature is pleasantly appealing.
Having a friend as loyal as you,
Will never allow me to feel blue.
When I think I have reached a dead end,
Who is there for me? You, my dear friend.
Many friendships don't last for long,
A disagreement takes place, the feeling is torn.
I pray that our friendship will hold,
Until we both become very old.

A Year in Time

The pleasant days of summer are gone,
There is a chill in the air, fall is here,
The leaves on the trees can no longer hold on,
Dropping off one by one,
Leaving the branches clear.
Squirrels scurrying around burying acorns,
Birds congregate in flocks and fly south.
The many plants that flowers did once adorn,
Have withered under Mother Nature's flout.
To witness this change can make one feel sad,
It happens every year, it's a temporary thing.
In a few short months we can all feel glad,
After fall and winter it will again be spring,
The months come and go, two plus ten,
New leaves on trees no more winter gloom.
Before we know it summer is here again,
The birds are back, flowers are again in full bloom.

The Loving Parent

Very young child is like a sapling tree,
That requires many hours of loving care.
It's a must to spend time and patience faithfully,
Someone to train and guide must always be there.
We all learn from our fathers and mothers,
Who wish to do for us what is best.
When the time comes for us to be among others,
Is when our training is put to the test.
If our parents have done their job well,
How we act and respect others will show.
All their hours of loving care will tell,
We will be people everyone will want to know.

Worth a Try

So many people live in despair,
And never think of saying a prayer.
It costs not a penny to kneel down and pray,
And ask God to hear what you have to say.
Some people think, as they sit and cry,
That it makes no sense to even try.
We are told that He will always care,
And that He will always be there.
He is not seen, He is in our mind,
He is never mean but always kind.
As sure as the day is twenty-four hours long,
It is a fact that His word is never wrong.
When people have faith in His word,
It is certain that their prayers will be heard.

Thinking of Peace

I overheard someone say,
What is wrong with people today?
They are no different than before,
They still go marching off to war.
Thinking this over in my mind,
I wonder if we are emotionally blind?
All wars that took place in the past,
Were supposed to be the very last.
Alas! When will all this chaos cease
To finally produce a truly lasting peace?

Nature's Power

No two people are born exactly the same,
Even identical twins, except for their last name.
Human minds invent new things every hour,
But are unable to control nature's power.
Truly amazing is Mother Nature's show,
A single drop of water turns into a flake of snow.
Among millions of flakes, no two are exactly the same,
Her awesome magic makes us humans seem lame.
She can hit us with many kinds of horrific weather,
And all we can do, is bear it and be tossed like a feather.
We will probably have to swallow our pride,
And continue to go along for the bumpy ride.

Why?

Why are so many people in such poor health?
Why do so many people have great wealth?
Why do so many people refuse to share,
While others show such loving care?
Why in this world live people who are so poor?
There are hundreds of thousands, to be sure.
Why do so many people just stand by,
And watch so many starve and die?
These questions have probably been asked
Throughout history,
If they will ever be answered, is still a mystery.

American Pride

Live life with pride, American pride,
Don't keep it all pent up inside.
Let it out! Let it out!
Don't be afraid, just shout it out.
This is America, our land,
By golly, isn't she grand?
She is surely the best,
She beats all the rest.
Let it out! Shout it out!
So great is America, from the inside out.

The Envy of the World

In America live people from every land,
That's why she has become so grand.
A great many came to escape from tyranny,
So that they can live in peace, forever free.
People are free to speak what they have to say,
And to the Lord, they are all allowed to pray.
Everyone is free to speak their mind,
Without fear of being shot from behind.
America is the envy of the world,
May all her freedoms be never spoiled.

Flying into the Future

As I laid there in my bed,
I heard a jet plane overhead.
Several dozen people in a flying machine,
A few hundred years ago it was just a dream.
It is amazing how that dream came true,
Since a time when it was only birds that flew.
In those days, only the horse could take us there,
Today in a fraction of time we can arrive by air.
We have now flown beyond our place,
And taken a spacecraft into outer space.

Memories

Many memories make us feel sad,
Some so sad, that they make us weep.
There are also many that make us glad,
They are the good ones that we will always keep.
On occasion something occurs bringing to mind,
Some sad incident that happened long ago.
The best thing to do is leave it behind,
And think about the good ones that we know.
It makes no sense to live in the past,
Since the past is forever gone.
The best way to make our happy ones last,
Is to look ahead and keep marching on.

God Is Your Friend

Life is never what it seems,
While we try to follow our dreams.
We wish to live without stress and strife,
But sad to say, that's not the way of life.
There are times when everything goes just right,
And we are happy all day and night.
There are also times when all we do goes wrong,
Then we begin to give up and feel forlorn.
That is when our faith is put to the test,
Either we feel doomed, or we try our best.
There is in everyone, a will to survive,
Surely we must recover to stay alive.
If at this time you feel that this is the end,
Try turning to God, for He is your friend.

The Birth of Jesus

Innocent children are born every single day,
Two thousand years ago someone special came our way.
He is the child Jesus, born of a virgin mother,
He is our Savior; there is no other.
He is the son of God the Father above,
Sent to us out of profound total love.
There was no big crowd to celebrate our Savior's birth,
Just some shepherds and wise men
Presenting incense and myrrh,
We hold him in our hearts so very dear,
And celebrate his birth at Christmas every year.

Christmas Tradition

Who brings toys to the children at Christmas each year?
Why! It's Santa Claus and his eight lovely reindeer.
He loves all the children who try hard to be good,
And those who listen to mom and dad as they should.
He's made his rounds on Christmas Eve for many a year,
With a sleigh full of toys and his trusted reindeer.
He doesn't care if they are rich or poor girls and boys,
He thinks of them all, by bringing them some toys.
The tradition of Christmas, loving and giving in peace,
Should go on forever, and never be allowed to cease.

Life Is Short

Moisture-laden clouds in the winter sky,
Can no longer hold on, crystals of ice begin to fly.
They fall and settle upon the earth below,
The many millions together form what we call snow.
It covers the ground for a very short stay,
When the sun shines strong it melts away.
Life in a sense, is like ice and snow,
How long it lasts, we just never know.
We work, love and live upon the earth,
It's normal; it's what we know since birth.
In time our life on earth melts like snow,
We can no longer hold on, we have to go.

Earth's Mysteries

Mother Earth, how many secrets do you hold,
How many will you allow mankind to behold?
You have witnessed millions of years of strife
Between so many different forms of life,
You produce molten lava deep within you
Then spurt it out to form land that is band new.
You are a haven to millions of different species,
Who thank you by covering you with their feces.
You can often become very violent
And cause great sorrow,
The greatest mystery to humans
Is what you will do tomorrow.

Grandpa's Buddy

(To Daniel James Kossmann)

Grandpa, may I sit upon your knee,
While you read children's stories to me?
Certainly my buddy, dear little boy,
You are precious to me, my pride and joy.
Grandpa, I have a question for you;
If I wasn't here what would you do?
The answer my child is an easy one,
I would pray to God for a precious grandson.
I've done that my buddy, this is true,
God heard my prayer and sent me you.

Despair to Repair

As we travel down the path of life,
We will encounter disappointment and strife.
We may think somehow we will never win,
But this is not the time to give in.
It is not the time to give in to despair,
It is the time to begin to repair.
Positive thinking should be the order of the day,
We cannot let positive thoughts get away.
It is never easy to follow this kind of advice,
It is not like throwing a roll of the dice.

The Lighthouse

Built upon a bed of stone,
I stand majestically all alone.
Throughout the night, and all day long,
During beautiful weather and terrible storm.
For many years sailors relied on me,
To shine my beacon of light over the sea.
My light is seen for many miles away,
Guiding so many vessels on their way.
Upon this tiny island I must forever be,
Helping many ships that sail upon the sea.
The seamen are happy that I stand upon this ground,
Making sure that they travel on safe and sound.

A Leaf in the Wind

Always being a very restless lad,
Has made his whole life so sad.
He would have so many different schemes,
Not exactly like having productive dreams.
Traveling from place to place,
In a crowd, just another face.
He just arrived in another town,
Seems he cannot settle down.
Drifting aimlessly in no apparent direction,
The clothes on his back, his only protection.
Like looking for something hidden on a shelf,
He just can't seem to find himself.
The day may come when drifting gives in,
And he will no longer be a leaf in the wind.

The Hurt

How confusing is this life that I live,
Deep in my soul feeling I have so much to give.
Day after day it's like an obstacle course,
Just beginning to gain ground, then another loss.
Should I have been born in a different time and place,
In a different body with a different face?
This nagging feeling deep within my soul,
Is slowly and surely taking its toll.
My efforts of well meaning are misunderstood,
By people who don't pay attention when they should.
I suppose as life goes on I may not win,
But not giving and caring would be a sin.

Simple Facts of Life

One last breath, a life is done,
It is gone like the setting sun.
Another life begins like the dawn,
An infant child is just born.
Every minute of every day,
Another life just fades away.
Like the morning's rising sun,
Another life has just begun.
Like the seasons that come and go,
The four of them, all of us know.
The ocean tides rise and fall,
This is all Mother Nature's call.
These facts are totally true,
Changing them; we cannot do.

A Letter

You were so irresistibly beautiful, then the tragic accident happened. You fell to pieces in such a way that no one thought that you could ever be as before. After many tedious hours were spent with tender loving care, you were whole once again. To everyone's surprise you are almost as good as new. You will never be exactly the same, but considering the terrible damage that you incurred, it certainly is a bit of a miracle that you are now in one piece. I will always stick by you until the end.

Affectionately,
Crazy Glue

P.S. Being such a pretty vase, it would be terrible if you were destroyed forever.

My Proverbs

A person who said that he never makes a mistake, just made his biggest mistake.

It would be great if a mind could mature with knowledge and at the same time retain the innocence of a child.

Words never cure the hurt. They can only soothe the profound pain.

Would you agree? If everyone were perfect, life would be awfully boring.

It is easy for me to find fault with you, the difficulty is in seeing my own faults.

If one must put another down to boost his ego, he proves that he is a fool.

Before you can fully digest success, you must first have a taste of defeat.